MY
CHILDREN ALONGSIDE
THE BATTLEFIELD

A COLLECTION OF REFLECTIVE SHORT STORIES
FROM A SINGLE MOTHER IN THE U.S. ARMY

VICKI DAVIS

ISBN: 978-0-578-73630-3
Library of Congress Control Number: 2020914738

Edited by Intuitive Enterprise Solutions
Book cover and layout design by Iskon Book Design
Photographs by @Tivoniart-Tivoni, Brundage

Dedication

THIS BOOK IS gratefully dedicated to my three children—Malcolm, Jalisa, and Charlie—whom I love with all my soul. You are the wind beneath my wings. You have been my inspiration to strive and be the best mom, person, and soldier that I can be in this world. Everything I have done in my life was for you.

I want each of you to know that I love you. I know at times it may have seemed that I was too hard on you. For that I am sorry. I was only trying to prepare you for this world. I am sorry that I was not always there for you. During all the times that I was absent from your life, there was not a day I did not think of you, did not miss you or pray for you.

I realize I made mistakes and I may have seemed distant at times. As a result, you may have felt neglected, unimportant, or alone. I am sorry, for those were never my intentions. You may have felt that I favored one of you more than the other. But I never did. You were all in different places in your life. I love all three of you the same.

I say to the three of you, "Thank you for loving me." I know I'm not the easiest person to love. And for you, as military children, I understand life was challenging, frustrating, and scary at times. Never having a place to call your own. Having to move every two or three years. Making friends only to turn around and say goodbye. It was all a real sacrifice. I salute all three of you, Malcolm, Jalisa, and Charlie, for your heroism in enduring all the challenges a military child has to bear. I love you with every fiber of my body.

I know there is so much more left unsaid. But if you did not know it before, then I trust you will know now that you are the greatest gift given to me by God in this world.

Love always and forever,
MOMMY

Contents

ONE

Rerouting

1

Take the Wheel

IT WAS A Friday morning. In the hours before sunrise, I woke with the heaviest of burdens on my chest. My eyes poured the weariness of my soul as my body moved to the edge of the bed and reached for my physical training uniform. It was mandatory Physical Training (PT) and I—the diligent, motivated soldier—never missed PT unless there was an emergency.

Muscle memory must have moved me to the car because, as I later attempted to mentally retrace my steps, I simply could not account for those 15 minutes of driving. I had always been an excellent navigator for the U.S. Army but maybe Jesus took the wheel that morning. I do not recall stopping at red lights or stop signs or showing my military ID card to guards on the base.

I arrived at my destination and put the car in park. I do not remember exiting the car or even deciding to reroute. I just remember walking in and smelling that strange hospital smell.

As I searched my psyche for answers, the soft tone of a woman in scrubs broke through my mental fortress. I realized that I had driven to the base hospital instead of the barracks for our First Sergeant meeting. Apparently, there was an emergency after all.

"How can I help you?" She was a nurse at the Blanchfield Army Community Hospital at Fort Campbell, Kentucky. I was not sure how long she had been asking or how long I had been struggling to respond. I looked at her, but no words would come out of my mouth. All I could do was cry.

"Are you hurt?" She asked a logical question since I had come in wearing my physical training uniform and weeping inexplicably. I felt pain but it was not physical. I had an *everything* ache.

"I just can't do this anymore," I said.

She asked me over and over again if I wanted to kill myself or someone else. I tried to hold a steady gaze, my eyes aimed in her direction, but I had no energy in my body or focus in my mind. I felt a deep sense of loss and had no words for it.

I shot a desperate glance at the woman as tears and mucus dripped off the bridge of my nose. I told her I needed help; I was having thoughts of committing suicide.

The doctor told the nurse to change me into a hospital gown and to get me a wristband. They called an ambulance for my transport.

That morning, Vanderbilt Psychiatric Hospital in Nashville, Tennessee, admitted me into their inpatient treatment program. They later diagnosed me with severe post-traumatic stress disorder (PTSD), military sexual trauma (MST), anxiety, and insomnia.

In treatment, I began to unpack some of the events that led up to the breakdown. I took inventory of my losses. The violent, bloody battles—out in the field and in my own home—had all contributed to what felt like the destruction of my sanity.

2

Sane Lies & Insane Truths

AFTER I WAS admitted, I told my three children I was away for training. I just did not want them to worry about me. Vanderbilt Hospital was about 45 minutes away from where we lived in Clarksville, Tennessee. The staff allowed me to make a few calls in order to make arrangements for their care.

I called my friend, Danna. We had gotten close when I had been stationed at Fort Campbell, Kentucky. The kids liked her and had fallen in love with her five-month-old baby boy. We were both senior leaders in the same brigade but different battalions.

Every Sunday I would cook dinner and she would come over and join us—along with other soldiers from the battalion. We ate and then played board games. We called each other by first names on the weekends. This was our way of letting our hair down. We knew that on Monday morning we had to go back to being professionals—addressing each other by rank and last names.

While she was pregnant, and after having her baby, Danna talked often of getting out of the Army so her parents could help her raise her baby. I told her she had already invested too much time in the Army and not to waste it.

In order to ease her load, I offered to watch the baby whenever she had 24-hour duty. I was always trying to help the soldiers who were also single mothers because I knew the difficulties firsthand. We called each other "battle buddies" because—in the Army— that means we always have each other's backs.

The day I called her from Vanderbilt Hospital, I had to decide how much I would tell her. In reality, I didn't know exactly what was going on with me or in my mind. When the words came to me, I finally told her I had been admitted into a "crazy hospital." Maybe I said that out of shame. Or maybe I feared scaring her off and not having anyone to watch my children. I tried joking to disguise my many emotions.

She did not laugh at all. She sounded very concerned for me and asked how she could help. I told her the doctor mandated I stay in the hospital for a while. Before I even asked, she offered to stay with the kids at my house. I did not know how long I would be there, but she assured me not to worry. She promised to stay as long as I needed her to. I thanked her and held my tears in.

Looking around the room, I noticed how it seemed almost as empty as I felt. It had two twin-sized beds (although I never had a roommate during my stay). The stark white walls were bare. The room had a bathroom, but the shower and sink had no plugs—maybe so that we would not drown ourselves? I had a door, but could not lock it.

The nurses would stop by every 30 minutes just to make sure I stayed safe. The hospital thrived on order and schedules. It was the same routine every single day for everyone in the same wing—just like a prison.

The nurses woke us up at 0700 hours in the morning. We had 30 minutes to get ready. There was breakfast and quiet time, TV time, lunch, and group therapy. Then we had our vital signs taken and were given our medication. Finally, there was visitation, dinner, and lights out. The only personalized thing was the appointments we had with our respective doctor.

I felt relief and a bit of gratitude that I did not have a roommate. It did not feel like the right place or the time to talk to anyone or even consider making friends. This way, no one heard how I cried myself to sleep at night from the agony of missing my children.

No one asked me what I could not stop asking myself: *How did I get here?*

I started attending group therapy sessions where people would talk about their sadness. At first, I would just listen. I did not participate at all. It did not feel right talking about such personal things with these people I had never met. The concept of group therapy was so foreign to me I was not even sure what it was or how it worked. I did not trust it.

I doubted that talking would fix anything and I begged to go home. The staff said I could only go home if the doctor approved my release. And the doctor did not think going home was in my best interest or in the best interest of my children. *My children.* He said I would have to stay longer if he did not see any improvement. I had to either open up or stay locked in there.

So, I talked.

Every day, for one hour, I would talk to a psychologist. She would ask me questions about what had happened during my deployments. When I went back to my room and met with that eerie quiet, I found myself alone with my thoughts—thoughts stirred and shaken from acknowledging the difficult truths I wanted to avoid. I drifted back to all the people I had lost through my deployments. I felt like a failure because I could not bring everyone back home to their loved ones.

The therapist even asked me about my childhood and a lot of questions about my personal life. I thought about *my own* children. Though they had never seen war, they had often suffered right alongside me.

Some days, after meeting with the therapist, I just could not shut my brain up. So, I would go to the dayroom and watch TV—sitting there quietly, hoping no one would speak to me, and waiting for medication time. After they gave us medication, I could rest.

I do not think I started to feel any better during my time at the hospital. As I spoke my truth, I thought I just sounded crazier and crazier to the doctors. I knew they would keep me longer if I kept telling them how things had gone; they did not understand what deployment was really like. But if I said nothing at all, I could not leave either. So, I decided to say what sounded reasonable. I knew what they wanted to hear.

Eight days after my sane lies replaced insane truths, they finally sent me home to my children with four types of medication and a treatment plan.

3

Winning the Battle, Losing the War

GETTING TREATMENT FOR my many diagnoses started to interfere with how much I loved my job. I had spent a lot of energy over the years trying to keep my work and my personal life separate. But that is especially difficult when you work where you live.

My Chain of Command came to visit me while I was in the hospital. I refused the visit because I felt embarrassed. My First Sergeant knew my diagnosis. Even my soldiers knew! It was no secret to them. It felt like suddenly everyone around me already knew—while *I* was still trying to figure it out.

What did it mean to devote 18 years to honorable service just to end up on medication and a treatment plan? Once they discharged me from the hospital, of course, I wanted to return to the place where I most belonged. At work, I had always felt pride in being useful and busy.

But that feeling did not return when I went back. Instead, that same embarrassment followed me around the office. I asked myself constantly, "How can a senior leader have PTSD? How can I lead soldiers?"

When I went for my first follow-up appointment, I only saw lower enlisted soldiers—including some from my unit. If you were sitting in *that* waiting room, people knew why you were there. The awkwardness of avoiding eyes kept most of us hanging our heads in shame.

My appointments took place during the day. Sometimes I would cancel just so that I could attend my unit meetings. More often, though, I cancelled just to avoid seeing the soldiers in the waiting room.

It felt strange to go back to work or training after having to relive traumatic events in my therapy sessions. Just the sight of dirt, rocks, and trees and I would forget that I was safe at home; that there were many miles between me *then*—fearing for my life on the battlefields of Iraq—and me *now*—enjoying the comforts of life on a military base. But in those moments, it all felt so close to me still. The fires. The shouts. The chaos.

A battlefield soldier with no rifle and no mission is forced to hear their own thoughts, to playback unpleasant memories, and sometimes even to create horrific new stories of their own. Certain smells would also do me in. Gunpowder from the range. Blood. I could not handle the scent of blood without thinking of unwelcome things.

After 21 years and 11 months of total service—with three of those years working while in treatment—I decided to retire. I did not even have a ceremony. I did not think anyone cared. I was not proud and did not feel like I had accomplished anything. What was there to celebrate? People were dead. And they were not coming back.

But maybe there was still time left to be there for my children. Two of them were still in high school and the other one had begun college. I could still be the mother my kids needed and deserved. The kind of mom who saw them off to the bus in the morning and who made it home before they got off the bus in the afternoon. The kind of mom who baked cookies. The kind of mom who participated in the PTA. No more deployments. No more uniforms. I wanted to make up for all the time I spent away from them.

I went to the Soldier Support Center office, picked up my DD214, and cried all the way home. An era had ended. War was all I had known since childhood. Perhaps now I could know peace.

4

∾

The 4 Team Take on Nashville Shores

O N JULY 4, 2012, all members of the 4 Team—
Malcolm, Jalisa, Charlie, and me—were
present and accounted for. Malcolm was 20, Jalisa
had just turned 19, while Charlie was 15. I called
us the 4 Team because we did not have much family
outside of us since divorcing Staff Sergeant (SSG),
Anthony three years earlier. Our little tribe literally
meant the world to me, and the struggles we had
endured together made us close over the years.

This newfound freedom I had after retiring
helped us all stretch our wings like fledging birds.
We had made plans to drive up to Nashville Shores
Waterpark in Hermitage, Tennessee. It would be our
first trip since my retirement from the U.S. Army

and nothing and no one could interrupt us. There would be no vehicle inspections, leave that needed approval, or senior leaders sending me places I did not want to go. We could do whatever we wanted and go wherever we wanted.

In the car on the drive down, we decided the 4Team would get together every Fourth of July. This would be our small family reunion and annual tradition.

Deep down, I wished for my children to be small again. They were the real heroes, not me. They had sacrificed so much and I wanted an award to recognize them with. Something that honored their bravery every time they had to leave behind their childhoods, their friends, and most of all—me—their only active parent. We were either a single parent family or a dual military family—where both parents are on active duty—for most of my career.

Often, when I reflect on all the things I missed because of my career, I am angry. But not that day. That day we all felt the magic of love and togetherness.

Nashville Shores is an amusement park and campground located near the banks of Percy Priest Lake. It was a beautiful day to lounge beside the crisp, blue wave pool while my kids enjoyed the colorful water slides.

Mostly, I recall my children's laughter. Malcolm made joke after joke and we laughed until our sides hurt. He pretended to be various famous people, so we made a game out of guessing whoever he impersonated. His facial expressions impressed us all. He could be so spot on!

After we left the waterpark, we decided to continue our day of fun at Dave and Buster's. We played arcade games, then sat together at a table talking about my children's plans for the future. I listened to their goals, their desires, their wishes, and I felt content. I looked forward to more of this and knew I had made the right decision in leaving the military. None of us could contain our excitement about this being a yearly family event. The possibilities felt endless.

"Can I drive back?" Malcolm asked. I told him yes, but I felt hesitant. Every single time Malcolm drove, the police always stopped him and pulled us over. Most young men Malcolm's age got in trouble for speeding and drove their parents crazy with high insurance rates. Not my son. Malcolm would get pulled over because he drove too slowly. I could tell this day was special, though, because we managed to make it all the way back without getting stopped.

"Well, it's about time," I teased Malcolm.

"What are you talking about?" he asked. We all erupted in laughter again.

"We didn't get stopped by the cops. That is a first," I told him.

Malcolm chuckled. "That's because now I am an expert driver."

I had always known my kids would be special.

5

My First-Born Son

NOT TOO LONG after I retired, Malcolm moved out of our family home. I missed Malcolm so much after he moved out that I began having dreams about him.

In one of my dreams, I saw Malcolm in a club. The people in the club started running because someone had a gun and opened fire. I walked over to where Malcolm stood in the club and held both of his hands. I looked straight into his eyes as he gazed into mine. I told him, "You do not have to run anymore. God has forgiven you of all your sins. God loves you." After I spoke those words, Malcolm faded away and I woke up.

Twenty-four hours after having that dream, I received a knock on my door. The clock said 05:58. It was a Saturday morning, November 3, 2012.

I answered the door. The gentleman knocking identified himself as a detective. In a deep voice, he said he had come to see me about my son. My heart dropped. Neither Malcolm nor Charlie were home at that moment. Charlie had stayed over at a friend's house the previous night. Malcolm had already moved out.

I quickly opened the door. "Who?" I asked him.

"Your son, Malcolm. He's been shot," the detective said. Everything became a blur.

I told the detective we should go to the hospital and then I dropped to the floor. I was home alone. Jalisa had also stayed at a friend's house. I could not really process what the detective had told me. I wanted to go to the hospital, but he would not let me leave the house.

I went to my room, got dressed, and asked the detective again if we could go to the hospital. He told me that I was not in any condition to see my son.

"I was a soldier for almost 22 years. I have seen it all," I told him.

He asked me to call someone to be there with me. I called my pastor, but the pain was still unbearable regardless of who was with me.

It did not matter that I had retired. It did not matter that I had promised Malcolm I would give him more hugs and kisses. The war had barged itself into my home once again.

And I blamed myself.

I was not the one who pulled the trigger, but I had missed all the times Malcolm needed me. It was truly too late. My sweet baby boy had been shot and killed.

~

I sat in the doctor's office processing his words.

"I know exactly what is wrong with you," he had said. "Congratulations! You are pregnant."

Suddenly, it all made sense in a funny way. Earlier that day, I weighed in overweight for the Army's height and weight standards and barely made it through my physical fitness test. Normally, I showed off when I took those tests. I loved working out and staying in shape. But after throwing up and feeling dizzy, I had been sent to the hospital to find out what was wrong with me.

I had felt so tired and sluggish, but I still had no idea I was pregnant. I do not think I even missed a cycle. But even if I did, my high level of physical activity made missing cycles fairly common.

When the shock wore off, I felt an overwhelming elation. I started talking to my baby in my belly. I made promises to love him, care for him, and give him two parents that would protect him. I told my baby I would never, ever give up on him no matter what he did—good or bad. Even at 19 years old,

I understood that I had been given the biggest responsibility in the world.

Before that moment, I had never wanted children. I figured I could just avoid all the pain from my childhood by not having any children of my own. But everything changed once I knew I was carrying a child of my own.

My next thoughts revolved around how I could manage being pregnant and staying in the Army. But a peace settled in my heart and I knew I could do it. I knew I was going to be a good mother—not because I had good role models—but because I knew what *not* to do. I could raise this child and give him or her all the love and time he or she needed from me.

I was going to teach my baby everything I had not been taught—valuable lessons about life, love, humbleness, compassion, and being the best person he or she could be. He would learn strength and the difference between right and wrong. I planned to protect my child until the day I died.

As I dreamed of the ideal life for my baby, I began to experience the bittersweet balancing act of motherhood and the military lifestyle.

Bitter because Malcolm's father, Junior, could not be stationed with me right away at Fort Huachuca, Arizona. We had decided to get married that coming November but were not married yet. So, this meant going to doctor's appointments alone.

Two weeks after getting the pregnancy results, I had an appointment with the OB/GYN for an ultrasound. When I first heard the heart rate on the monitor, I thought something was wrong. The heartbeat was so fast! But the doctor reassured me that the beats per minute looked normal and the baby looked healthy. I cried tears of pure happiness then.

Bitter also because my peers got mad when they had to take on some of my workload. My commander at that time gave me a counseling statement explaining my limitations due to pregnancy. But I still had to perform physical training, details, and 24-hour duty. I still had to show up to formation and do some of the exercises with the unit. There was no post-pregnancy PT or "sections" as they have now.

One day, I heard other soldiers and seniors talking about me.

"She's so lucky. She doesn't have to do anything," they said. They were mad that I could not do everything they were doing. I did not "look" pregnant while in uniform for most of my pregnancy. I do not recall wearing any pregnancy uniforms until the third trimester.

Some of my senior leaders tried to put me on duty that would have been too hard, physically, for me and the baby. I constantly had to show them my profile paperwork from the commander proving my pregnancy.

Pulling 24-hour duty especially wore me out. It was not until I was about eight months pregnant that I stopped doing overnight shifts. Before that, the supervisors would often send me home early from work because I could barely stay awake. I imagined that it looked like I received special treatment. Although I did not like getting singled out, there were definitely some pregnancy perks that I enjoyed.

One time while on post driving back to my apartment, the post police stopped me. The officer walked towards my car and leaned forward.

"I'm stopping you because you were speeding," he grunted. I was scared because, if you got a ticket on post, they notified your Chain of Command and put points on your license. The officer leaned a bit closer to me through the window.

"Oh, I see you are expecting," he sang, the tone of his voice changing completely.

"Yes, Sir," I said.

"Are you speeding because you have to use the bathroom?"

Of course, I said, "Yes."

"I'm not going to give you a ticket. Just stay under the speed limit. And congratulations! Take care and stop speeding."

~

My first son was born December 31, 1991, in Fort Ord, California. I named him Malcolm Rashaad Wright. Malcolm after Malcolm X—the strongest most fearless leader I had ever read about. I followed Malcolm X's work and admired him.

His middle name came from Phylicia Rashad. She was my TV mother. I saw her as the smartest, most talented, and phenomenal woman in the world. I knew that by naming my son after these two powerful people, he would be someone important in this world.

He was the smallest little person I had ever seen the first time I held in my arms. He was so teeny I feared I would break him. He weighed five pounds and 11 ounces. I felt glad to have a baby boy. I never knew the gender for sure until the day of his birth. But I felt in my heart he would be a boy and had only picked a boy's name.

The Army allowed me 45 days of convalescent leave. Convalescent leave permitted me to bond with him, heal, and enjoy motherhood. But 45 days just did not feel like enough time.

Begrudgingly, and far too soon, I enrolled my newborn baby in daycare. Being a mommy *and* a soldier on my own meant waking up at 0400 hours in the morning to get my baby ready for drop off at daycare just to make it on time for PT formation that started at 0600 hours.

During my lunch break, I rushed over to the daycare to spend lunch with my baby. I would get so excited after work because I knew I would see him soon.

Malcolm did not sleep much at night, so I felt exhausted and sleep deprived all the time. But I did not mind the extra effort. It was all for him. For the first time in my life, I really felt unconditional love; not just my love for him but him loving me back without even trying. It was the most natural thing I had ever felt.

I truly saw him as precious—he learned something new and grew so fast every day! I loved being a mom to my baby. I enjoyed the fact that I was not alone anymore. Motherhood, just like being a soldier, suited me.

TWO

Backtracking

6

Soldier First

To the Army, I was a soldier first. I volunteered to live, breathe, drink, eat, and smell the Army. Considering the home, I had come from, I agreed to this arrangement happily.

Growing up, my life had often been about secrets and survival. I trusted no one and had very few friends. I was somewhat of a loner—even inside my family. I felt okay with that; I knew I was different.

When I saw the movie *Full Metal Jacket* in my junior year of high school, it all clicked. I saw the world as a very unsafe place. But I figured my upbringing made me tough and prepared me well for a life dedicated to defending my country.

When the recruiters came to William L. Dickinson High School in New Jersey, I attended the meeting and took the Army Service Vocational Aptitude

Battery (ASVAB) test. Four weeks later, I reported to the Military Entrance Processing Station (MEPS) in New Jersey to officially swear in and join the Army.

I felt scared but excited to leave my childhood behind. I thought I would finally have total control of my life! I thought no one would hurt me ever again. I felt free.

The Army made sure to drill into us some important messages on leadership right away. I vividly remember the day we learned how to throw grenades over a tall brick wall. It was November of 1989 at Fort McClellan, Alabama.

My 18-year-old mind had showed up to bootcamp empty and ready to receive orders. My athleticism allowed me to excel quickly above my peers in weaponry and obstacle courses. But as accomplished as I felt, as I got to know a new side to myself in bootcamp, nothing compared to the leadership of those drill sergeants. I started to gain a lot of respect for the drill sergeants because they voluntarily risked their safety to lead us daily.

We threw live grenades in training. That meant if the grenades did not make it over the wall, the drill sergeant could be seriously injured or even killed. They did this day in and day out with their new recruits.

Everything the drill sergeant taught us to do, they could do too. The people teaching us did not just sit safely behind a desk. To me, it felt like walking in the footprints of giants. I admired them as much as I respected them. Through them, I learned to always put my soldiers before myself.

In the early days of my career with a 111 Military Intelligence Brigade, the soldiers' sacrifice came natural to me. I already lived a life with minimal distractions and intense focus. I did not socialize much, though the military atmosphere seemed similar to college—lots of partying, drinking, and staying up late.

My battle buddies joked and called me "gay" because I did not date or sleep with different men like they did. I had not dated anyone in high school either. I did everything alone and felt content simply because I had my job and my goals. Just like the slogan, I wanted to be all I could be!

I performed well at my job. I actually only ever met Junior because I'd earned an opportunity to take advanced training for six weeks in Fort Ord, California, after getting promoted to the next rank. Junior became the first person I had ever actually dated.

I loved every single thing about the freedom and opportunities the Army provided to me—at least until I had Malcolm. Suddenly, I felt split in two. Malcolm had given me a family, a real family—something I never thought I could have. From the first moment

I held him, I felt compelled to develop a foundation of security, dependability, trust, and unconditional love for my family. I felt like I had a new priority outside the Army.

Upon my return to work after having Malcolm, my boss placed me on duty immediately. I had not yet found anyone to keep my son in the evenings, but he made it clear that I would get written up if I didn't show up for duty.

"The Army did not issue you a family," he stated, "This is your problem." That was the moment I began to realize what it truly costs to be a soldier first.

7

Korea: The Hardship Tour

I USED UP EVERYTHING in me to push back the tears. They did not understand what Mommy told them. I looked into their sweet faces. I imagined them waking up and looking for me or crying out for me. The thought broke my heart. I could only leave behind a picture of myself and hope they would remember me.

I have experienced much adversity but none quite like leaving my then two-year-old son, Malcolm, and 17-month-old daughter, Jalisa, for the first time.

I had evaded this assignment once before—out of sheer luck or divine intervention, I am not sure. The first time, a mere three months after giving birth to Malcolm, the Army assigned me to Korea for a year without dependents. I felt like I had to do something. There was no way I would leave my newborn child.

I asked my Chain of Command if they could stop this assignment, but they told me having a baby does not exempt anyone from their obligations. I had to fulfill the assignment or get kicked out of the Army. I was devastated. I had made a promise to protect Malcolm!

I called Junior, crying, to tell him about my assignment to Korea. I told him I thought it would be best if I just got out of the Army so I could take care of the baby. Junior sat silently on the other end of the phone for what felt like an eternity.

"That's just not possible," Junior finally said. He explained he was going through the legal process for evading the cops on his second DUI. Soon, he would be kicked out of the Army and he planned to come stay with me in Fort Huachuca, Arizona.

I angrily hung up on him and just held my baby tightly. *The second DUI?* I fumed to myself. *Not even the first one.* It started to sink in that I had married a stranger. I tried again to get out of the assignment, but ultimately, I would have to go, and I would need to find someone to keep my baby.

Obviously, Junior should have been my first choice, but he had not been much help with Malcolm during convalescent leave and now he seemed to have a drinking problem. I did not feel secure, but I wasn't sure what other choice I had. I stayed married to Junior just to make sure someone would be around to keep Malcolm during my time in Korea.

Two days before I would have left for Korea, I was visiting friends in Georgia when I found out I was pregnant again. This made me ineligible for the assignment to Korea.

They directed me to the nearest base instead— Fort Benning, Georgia—where my daughter was born on February 10, 1993. Something about moving there refreshed me in a way I did not know I needed. I liked our life in Georgia so much that I bought a house there. Perhaps it was me feeling at home with my little family that helped me throw away the pieces to the puzzle that did not fit.

I saved up enough money to get a lawyer and divorced Junior soon after Jalisa was born. The infatuation I had felt in those six weeks of training at Fort Ord, California had definitely run its course.

The year or so we actually lived in the same house as husband and wife, I didn't feel much like a wife. He frequently had affairs, it took him too long to find a job after getting kicked out of the Army, and he did not help much around the house. The heavy drinking also continued. He did not meet my expectations as a husband or a father.

It had been hard enough being responsible for one baby while preparing to bring another one into the world at the tender age of 20. But the realization that my husband was just an old baby hit me the hardest. *I cannot deal with the old baby,* I thought to myself; *the old baby has got to go!*

Divorcing Junior and gaining full custody of Malcolm and Jalisa gave me renewed focus at work. Junior was one less mouth to feed so I knew I would be okay. I did not let that setback stop me. I put all my energy and time into my children and career.

I wanted to make it to the next rank of E-5, which required much more of me. I began studying for the promotion board. The Army uses a board panel to determine if a soldier is ready to move up or not. At the E-5 board, the board members asked questions to make sure I knew how to be a leader. I did extremely well; I even maxed the board.

Then, I took college courses at Troy State University for an associate degree. I did everything I needed to get to the next rank. But that took me away from my children more than I wanted. I left for 30 days just to complete the Primary Leadership Development Course (PLDC).

As a newly single mother with two children, it became especially important for me to have reliable help with them. When the orders for Korea came around again a few months after the divorce, Junior was still on my Family Care Plan. In the Army, single parent families and dual military service member families must submit a written agreement for their dependents called a Family Care Plan. The plan grants caregivers the power of attorney whenever soldiers are deployed or on assignment for an extended period of time. This empowers caregivers to make decisions regarding medical care, schooling, and anything else that may arise in order to take care of the children.

It works a lot like granting legal guardianship. There is even an allotment with an agreed dollar amount set up for the caregiver that gets deducted directly from the soldier's pay. This agreement always stays drafted and ready to execute. It is audited annually to ensure the plan remains active and all parties involved agree. Soldiers must be ready to defend our country with no excuses! If you did not have a Family Care Plan in place, you would be kicked out of the Army for lack of adequate family care.

Most soldiers I knew had family members helping with their children. I often had to find close friends to help me. I did not have much family ... and the family that I did have would not help me with my children. Asking their fathers was never as simple as it sounded.

I was really afraid to ask my ex-husband to keep the children. If he said no, I had no clue what to do next. Junior agreed to keeping Malcolm and Jalisa for the 12 months, but it came with some demands. I had to pay him $600.00 dollars for the allotment and allow him to stay in my home rent-free. My hands were tied. I did not have anyone else reliable to call on at the time.

Once a caregiver agrees to all the responsibilities, they must also understand that anything can happen during training, tours, and deployments. A soldier's time away can be extended with little to no notice or something terrible could happen, like a near-fatal injury or even death. I knew Junior's motivation to help for an entire year was not our children, so whenever he got nasty, I would offer him more money. I was willing to live meagerly so my children could thrive back home with their father.

While in Korea, I often felt bitter about the separation from my babies. Not everyone on the tour had to be without their dependents. I wished I could have just taken my children with me! While I logically understood the reason—going on a tour with your dependents required more rank than I had at the time—this fact never sat well with me emotionally. I wonder if this fueled my desire to go for the highest rank a female could make in 1994. (I must make that distinction because women were not allowed to work in field artillery.)

I am not sure if this was my reasoning, but I do know my time in Korea—though lonely—solidified the Army as my sole career path. I fell back into my old habits quickly without my children around and threw myself into my work.

After the fiasco with Junior, I definitely did not want to date. And I still could not bring myself to trust anyone there. I watched my colleagues lie almost daily. It seemed to me that people took our TDY or "temporary duty for a year" to mean something closer to "temporarily divorced for a year." So, my social life and Korean cultural experience consisted largely of my work interactions with the Korean Augmentation to the United States Army (KATUSA) soldier assigned to me as well as other local soldiers I met along the way. Conversations about our differences with KATUSA soldiers entertained me and distracted me from missing my children.

With the 11-hour time difference and their ages, I could not speak to them much. I would call, but Junior did not always answer the house phone. And even when he did, small children do not necessarily want to sit in front of a phone.

About halfway through the tour, I saved up enough money to come home for Christmas, meaning I would also be home for Malcolm's third birthday.

As the plane landed, my excitement to see my children peaked. My family stood there waiting for me at the gate. Junior set Jalisa down and I waited, kneeling, to hug my little ones.

"There she goes, right there," Junior said to Jalisa—pointing in my direction.

"Where is my mommy?" she managed, running right passed me. She did not even recognize me. It took hours before she would come to me. And when she did come, she did not come to me excited. Sometimes, a child will go to a relative or friend if you say, "Go give them a hug." They will go, but they are scared. You can tell they obeyed only because you told them to. That is how it was with Jalisa. It served as a heartbreaking reminder of just how much I had missed in my daughter's second year.

Seven months into the Korea tour, I received my promotion to sergeant E-5. I had done it! It felt good to at least have my many sacrifices rewarded.

8

Specialist Abigor

Fort Eustis, Virginia, was my first duty station as a sergeant and a single mom. When I returned from Korea, the Army reassigned me so I could not go back to Fort Benning, Georgia. I begged the Army to send me back to Fort Benning, but the answer was no. I *had* to relocate.

I moved into military housing, got both children enrolled into daycare, and began working with the USAALS 1st 765th Transportation Battalion at Fort Eustis, Virginia.

Virginia was a beautiful state, but I had left my heart in Georgia. A few months after moving to Virginia, a friend I knew from back home in Jersey City, New Jersey, moved in with me on the base. I had run into Kelly by chance while out and about on a weekend trip back home. We had gone to high school together and she had been one of the only people I spent time with outside of school. We got to talking and Kelly revealed she needed a place to stay. I just so happened to need help with the children.

She ended up driving back to Virginia with me the next day. It was not something we really thought out. She was in need and I was in need.

Kelly and I got along pretty well. She looked after Malcolm and Jalisa while I worked. She did well with the children, and I did not have to get up early to drop them off at daycare anymore. We were both in our early twenties, though, and I do not think she wanted to spend all day, every day, in the house.

Soon after she moved in, I met the neighbor next door, a single soldier, Specialist Abigor. Specialist Abigor was 6'3", green eyed, light skinned, and he wasn't in my unit. I never dated anyone in my unit! (If you date them and break up, then life really sucked.)

Specialist Abigor offered to do small favors for me—cut the grass, wash my car, fix things around the house. I found him attractive and he talked smoothly, telling me how pretty I was.

I invited Specialist Abigor over for dinner one night. And after that, he pretty much became part of my world. Looking back, I realize it felt good to have someone paying me some attention. I was single, divorced, and had two children. Most of all, I felt afraid to be on my own. I believe that is why I invited Specialist Abigor into my life without really knowing him.

"I don't like him," Kelly said. He had a rough, gruff way about him that turned Kelly off.

"You don't know him. Give him a chance," I answered. "He's just a military guy."

I also saw what Kelly saw, but I understood how the military is a man's world. I accepted the rough talk from military men more than from civilian men because there were places in the military without women around at all, places where men could completely be themselves. Even when those military men got around women, they still acted and talked rough. They just could not tone it down.

As the Army has progressed over the years, things have changed. But in the '90s, it was not a place for emotions or sensitivity. I understood this because I had my own struggles with showing emotion. Kelly was a civilian. She did not understand anything military-related, and I never took the time to explain it to her.

It did not take Kelly long to move back to Jersey City once Specialist Abigor and I started dating. Whenever he came around, she went to her room. When she left for good, I quickly saw a different side to Specialist Abigor.

It started with him asking me for things—little things at first like gas money and then bigger things like tires for his car. As long as I gave him what he wanted, he continued to say nice things to me. But when I said no, I was "useless," "dumb," and "ugly." It is like he knew exactly what to say to trigger memories of my childhood. My father had always called me those things too. And I had believed it because it was my father telling me those things.

I did not like Specialist Abigor asking me for money. I felt that, as a single mom, he should have been helping me!

Specialist Abigor progressed from mental to physical abuse within two months of Kelly leaving. The physical started with shoving and grabbing. And then punching and hitting. Meanwhile, he increased his demands and his threats. He wanted to move in with me and tell his Chain of Command that he lived off post so he could collect his housing benefit. He wanted me to go to work and come straight home. He did not want me to have any friends. He convinced me that he watched me all the time.

Then, he showed me his gun. I do not know where he got this gun from. It was not an Army-issued weapon. He wanted me to know exactly how he planned to kill me and my children. If I refused him anything—anything at all—he became violent. I felt like a prisoner of war in my own home.

I narrowly avoided moving in with Specialist Abigor simply because he got into a fight at a stoplight that got him arrested. He stayed locked up for a few weeks. When law enforcement released him, the Army found out that he had been lying to keep his housing. The Army believed he had children and a wife. But he had gotten a divorce and I never saw his children at his home. Once they found out, they expected him to live in the barracks. He often drove out to visit me.

With bruises as evidence on my arms, I opened up to a fellow Soldier—a woman who I enjoyed talking to while at work. She did not know how to help me. It still shocks me to this day that she had no idea what to do. I also did not know who *else* to talk to, so the problems continued.

One particular night, he rang the doorbell. I had just put my children to bed and was dressed in my nightgown. I tried to ignore the ringing, but then the banging started.

I wanted the banging to stop and I definitely did not want to wake up my children. I believe he knew that. Eventually, I opened the door and Specialist Abigor walked right in.

"Please leave," I asked him.

I hoped I would just ask him to leave and he would leave. He did not. He headed to the bedroom. I followed. I whispered sharply to him, raising my arms to emphasize that I wanted him to leave. He grabbed both of my arms and threw me on the bed. He raped me for the first time that night.

I cried myself to sleep. But somewhere in my mind, I felt like I deserved everything he did to me.

Most of my concern went to my children. I did not want them to see or know that Specialist Abigor continued to abuse me physically, mentally, and sexually. As the result of one sexual assault or another, I ended up pregnant with Specialist Abigor's child.

At some point during my pregnancy, my First Sergeant called me into his office. He let me know it had come to his attention that I had not paid my Army Deferred Payment Plan (DPP) credit card bill. This was a huge problem and did not look good, but I did not even know that my credit card had been used at all! I had to put together who had done this right there in his office. I realized Specialist Abigor had stolen my credit cards and ran up the bills. And I knew it was him because the bill showed usage in Specialist Abigor's hometown of Cleveland, Ohio.

I opened up to my First Sergeant and I told him about the abuse going on at home. He told me to stop being irresponsible, making up excuses, and lying.

"Go pay your bills," he said.

I will never forget driving home and crying the whole way there. I felt alone in the world. The Army was not there for me and now I had no idea what else to do. If there was an Army protocol for women getting abused, I did not know it as a new sergeant.

When I came home to confront Specialist Abigor about the credit cards, he hit me so hard I fell on the floor in the middle of the hallway. Specialist Abigor jumped on top of me and started punching my pregnant belly from side to side. I remember Malcolm coming down the stairs.

"Go back upstairs," I yelled, "Everything is okay. I will be up soon. Just go back to bed." I did not mean to yell at him, but I was trying to protect him. Specialist Abigor threatened to kill all three of my children that night. I knew no one would come to save me. I prayed for a way out.

~

I ended up having my youngest son, Charlie, three weeks early.

"After you have this baby, I'm going to get you pregnant again," Specialist Abigor whispered in my ear menacingly as I tried to concentrate on bringing a healthy baby into this world. During labor, the doctors wanted to get my blood pressure down and steady the baby's heart rate. But my mind was already on preventing my next pregnancy.

Two weeks after giving birth to Charlie, I went to my follow-up appointment with the doctor.

"How is everything going?" he asked.

"Fine. Can you please tie my tubes?"

"But you are too young," he objected.

He was right. I was only 25 years old at the time. But I begged him.

"Are you sure?"

"Yes," I assured him. "Please."

He agreed to do it but kept asking if I was sure. I really did not feel certain; I just felt scared of what Specialist Abigor would do to me. I could not tell my doctor that part. My doctor was a man and I did not think he would care. None of the other men in my life seemed to care. The only thing I knew for sure: I did not ever want to get pregnant by this abusive, controlling man again!

After pleading with the doctor, he scheduled me for tubal ligation surgery. I felt extremely sad once they finished. But I believed it was the best thing for me at the time.

Something about my baby boy Charlie made me forget, even if just for a little while, the reality of the situation I found myself in with Specialist Abigor. Once I brought the baby home, he was such a joy to me and the kids. Both Malcolm and Jalisa loved their roles as older siblings.

But our joy did not last. Specialist Abigor repeatedly threatened to take Charlie and disappear. Since he gave Charlie his last name, Specialist Abigor convinced me that in the state of Virginia I had no real rights to my baby. I had 45 days during convalescent leave to figure out what to do about childcare. But on day 46, I had to go back to work.

I did not want Charlie in a daycare.

That left Charlie vulnerable for Specialist Abigor to take him. The Army planned to kick Specialist Abigor out soon because of the fight he had gone to jail for. That would only make it easier for him to run away with my son. He rarely made empty threats, so I believed everything he told me.

I ended up taking Charlie to a co-worker to keep him while I worked. She was a great person who had just retired from the Army, and her rates were very affordable. I knew she would keep my baby safe at her home. She agreed that only I could pick him up and no one else. I made that very clear to her! Since she lived close to the base, I always went to her house on my lunch breaks so I could spend time with my baby. Fear had me constantly checking on his safety.

After all the praying and trying to leave, a way out finally came. I was shopping at the Commissary when I ran into an old acquaintance from Korea. Sergeant Jones told me he had come back home to Virginia because his father had just passed away from cancer. I did not even know he was from Virginia.

I could see the grief in his eyes. It felt good for both of us to see a friendly, familiar face. We spoke for hours about the good times in Korea and the people we both knew. I remember he had a crush on me in Korea, but at that time I was just focused on getting back to my children.

Eventually, I cut our conversation short. I had to get back home before Specialist Abigor became angry. But we agreed to meet a couple of days later at my office to catch up.

When we talked, the conversation lasted for hours and we talked about everything. I had noticed his rank when we first ran into one another and knew he was not doing too well in the Army. He had been demoted. Without me asking, he explained his father's terminal cancer and how his unit would not let him come home to be with his father. He started a fight that earned him an Article 15. Then, the Army discharged him.

A couple of days after he finally made it home, his father passed. He also confided in me about the loss of his mom and daughter. It was heartbreaking to hear his story

"So, what is going on with you?" He asked. "I see you got a baby, but you look empty inside." He could tell I had no joy despite baby Charlie.

"You can trust me. I will not judge. I'm only here to listen and help if I can." He had a very soothing voice. I felt reassured. I opened up again about Specialist Abigor. Sergeant Jones came up with a plan to help. And I agreed to take it.

Sergeant Jones stopped by the house and confronted Specialist Abigor. He told him if he did not leave me alone, he would call the cops.

"You will never again put your hands on her!"

Specialist Abigor left my house but as he walked out, the threats continued.

"You gonna get yours," Specialist Abigor said to me. He also yelled about taking Charlie away from me again. He was good at hitting me and yelling at me, but when another man confronted him, he acted like a coward. Specialist Abigor left my house that day without it getting physical.

Sergeant Jones stopped by the house every evening for months to ensure our safety. Specialist Abigor stopped coming by but he kept calling with threats of taking my baby. At the same time, he never asked to see Charlie. And of course, he never helped out financially.

A couple of weeks later, Sergeant Jones asked me to marry him. He figured he could best protect me, Charlie, and the kids that way. Sergeant Jones told me he planned to legally adopt Charlie to keep him safe from Specialist Abigor. I really did not know what to do because I was not in love with or even attracted to Sergeant Jones. I knew I needed to do something else to ease my fear, so I decided to marry Sergeant Jones. I was not sure if that was the right thing to do, but the fear for my children's lives controlled every move I made at this time.

First, we went to the Justice of the Peace and got married. Then, we went to the library courthouse and typed up the petition for Sergeant Jones' legal adoption of Charlie. Before the court approved and finalized the paperwork, we had to put it in the newspaper. Charlie's biological father, Specialist Abigor, had 30 days to dispute the petition. Specialist Abigor never came forward.

After 30 days, my new husband became Charlie's legal father and gave him his last name. Charlie would never *need* to know what an awful father he had. But even with the adoption, I knew that one day I would have to tell Charlie the truth about his birth father. In the back of my mind I also worried that Malcolm or Jalisa would tell Charlie about the terrible man they watched beat on their mother. They never did. I believe they wanted to protect their little baby brother.

With the paternity issues settled, Sergeant Jones, the kids, and I moved to a place where Specialist Abigor could not find us. I finally had peace. Sergeant Jones promised to give me and all my children a better life. I never knew a man could be so kind, loving, and gentle with children that were not even his.

9

*All You Must Hold
Onto is You*

SERGEANT JONES HAD a way with my children that touched my heart, but it did not create romantic feelings. Our marriage was more like an arrangement for security and protection.

When I terminated the marriage after only two years, I terminated my most reliable help. I wrote the check, but guilt paid for the divorce ... and for the car that Sergeant Jones drove away in as he left our lives. Pride prevented me from asking for child support, since he was not Charlie's biological father.

I had continued paying a mortgage for our home in Georgia as well as rent in Virginia. I think I just kept hoping, eventually, that I could move my family back to Georgia. But I was barely financially afloat after paying all the bills for both homes, two vehicles, and the credit card debt left by Specialist Abigor.

Only a couple of weeks after the divorce I found out about my promotion to the next rank. In spite of such a great accomplishment, the joy could not reach my heart. In frustration, all I felt was a tangled web of emotions. It was hard to unravel my worry about money from my enthusiasm about the promotion. I needed money to go make money or I would lose the money I had not made yet! I had no time or energy to figure everything out.

My poor diet caught up with me. I had been so focused on feeding the kids that I had not been feeding myself. My weight was as low as my energy. The pantry, fridge, and cabinets mirrored the emptiness I felt on the inside. I had hit rock bottom. I had two chicken thighs in the fridge, a container of rice in the pantry, and no money.

I fed the kids chicken and rice and wearily cleaned up after dinner. Malcolm was nine, Jalisa was eight, while Charlie was only three. They never knew their mommy never ate dinner that night. After the dishes, I put away my pride. I decided to call Malcolm and Jalisa's father, Junior, for help. But Junior had no money and even less concern for his children's well-being.

When that did not work out, I thought about who else I could ask. I landed on a battle buddy from bootcamp. We were never the best of friends, but we had been stationed together at almost every duty station since I was 18 years old. She was a hard worker and loyal soldier.

After I asked her if I could borrow $300.00 dollars, she did not say yes right away. Although it didn't come naturally to me, I decided to be vulnerable and honest, and told her why I needed the money. She hesitated for a moment and then, finally, told me yes.

"Just stop by the house tomorrow and I will give it to you," she said. I did just as she asked. But when I stopped by, she told me that she had decided not to lend me the money. I was shocked.

"Thanks," I responded and walked quickly back to my car. I did not want her to see me crying. My emotions of shame and sadness were intense.

God must have heard my calls for help. The very next day, I received an advance direct deposit into my account. The Army intended the money to cover school expenses, including food and travel expenses to get me to school for the first day and to return home on the last day. Instead, I used the money to buy groceries, pay the sitters, and pay for daycare.

I bought myself ten-cent packages of ramen noodles. At 5'4", I weighed 105 pounds. I suffered from chronic diarrhea because of malnourishment. But the children were well taken care of. That is all that mattered to me.

Going through financial hardships reinforced some of the ideas I had about life from childhood. I already did not trust anyone. As much as I knew I could use help, I did not find the kind of help I wanted. The Army had always required high levels of sacrifice. So, I had gotten used to giving things up.

I knew if I just sacrificed the house in Columbus, Georgia—something I could always replace—I would have more discretionary income. Ultimately, I lost the house to a foreclosure. I was okay with the foreclosure though, because I could go back to building a good life for my kids.

Through the financial and emotional fire, I faced, I promised myself I would never be in the position where I had to borrow money again. I did not want to experience that deep shame and sadness ever again. I have kept the promise to this day.

10

Together, We Stand

IN 2001, WHILE working at Fort Eustis, Virginia, the Army reassigned me to the 71st Transportation Battalion as the battalion supply sergeant. I felt excited and proud because this was the highest position I had ever held. The new assignment came with more responsibility and involved rubbing shoulders with higher ranking personnel.

Things went well until I met Command Sergeant Major (CSM), Real the Battalion CSM. He was about six feet tall and he had brown skin with a lot of grey hair in his ears. He would always come into my office to check on his soldiers. Initially, he asked me a lot of supply questions. I accepted his presence and did not mind updating him on how his soldiers worked— despite the fact that I had already spoken to his supply sergeant.

Before long, though, I began to feel uncomfortable when he would ask personal questions like if I had a boyfriend, if I liked to drink, or if I wanted to go out with him. I already did not like the CSM's personal questions. Then he started bringing me presents. When he spoke to me, he moved too close. Sometimes he even placed his hand on top of my hand. I hated him touching me or invading my personal space.

On one such occasion, I sat at my desk, head down, glued to my computer. I had to finish my hand receipts before I went home. I was the last person in the office. The CSM quietly maneuvered his way to my cubicle. I looked up when he sat down in the chair next to my desk.

"You look tense," he told me in a low tone. He was right. I was focused on getting these hand receipts finished before morning. His presence distracted me. He proceeded to offer me a body massage and placed his hands on my shoulders.

"I have to close the office," I announced and leapt to my feet. He had undoubtedly crossed the line.

"Let me take you to dinner," he offered. I declined.

Eventually, I started to leave my office and hide when he came around. I hated working with him. I felt afraid on the job. Because of his rank, I did not tell anyone. I was just a staff sergeant—an E-6. I did not think anyone would believe me. I also did not have much faith in the sexual harassment program

They had a male soldier in charge of the program at that time.

A fellow soldier, a female, saw me make a mad dash to the bathroom one day. This aroused her suspicions and she began asking questions.

"Are you okay? I saw you practically run in here."

"Running from CSM Real," I replied before I realized what I had said.

Her expression showed concern, and her tone softened as she leaned in. "Why?" she asked quietly. I did not want to worry a junior soldier, so I played it off.

"Oh, no," I tried to laugh it off. "I'm good. I'm straight."

A few months later, an investigating general officer came in to ask me questions about the CSM. The investigator wanted to know if the CSM had harassed me. They requested that I write a statement on a complaint form about the events that had taken place.

Because of the investigation, I learned there had been others. Apparently, he had been harassing three other women in the brigade. I felt thankful the concerned soldier from the bathroom had given my name to the investigator.

This time, our combined testimonies impacted change. The Army released the CSM from his duties. Although the Army let him retire, they had still gotten rid of him. It was unprecedented at the time that they believed me and the other junior enlisted soldiers over a male senior leader. When my father had violated me as a child, no one—not even my mother—stood up for me. But CSM Real's removal felt like a personal and professional victory.

As a woman in the Army, I constantly felt disrespected by the male leadership. However, this situation showed me the power we could have over a corrupt system.

In the end, I opted to take the Equal Opportunity Leaders Course (EOLC). Graduates of EOLC qualify to assist with informal equal opportunity complaints. The EO complaints dealt with issues related to discrimination based on things like race and gender. I felt honored to become part of the solution.

THREE

You Have Arrived

11

Operation Iraqi
Freedom: Part I

S EPTEMBER 11, 2001, changed military
operations forever. I left that day on a mission
to pick up supplies for my unit. The manager of
Sam's Club asked if I could go to the rear of the
store with him where they kept the television in their
break room.

"Look what just happened," he said. I watched
what was happening on television and could not
believe my eyes. The terrorist attack on the twin
towers had taken place not even 15 miles from my
hometown. As I left the store with my coworker, all
the customers looked at us with fear in their eyes.
Their gazes pled for answers from us because we
wore uniforms. It made sense that they would look

to us; in reality, we felt just as scared and confused as they were.

I rushed straight to my children's schools and picked them all up. I tried to call my supervisor. I tried getting in touch with people from back home in Jersey City, but all the phone lines had gone down. Like many Americans, I spent the day clutching my children in front of the television, watching the news, and trying to make sense of things.

The attacks were not something I *just* watched on television, however. I felt directly impacted. In the aftermath of the attacks, I was angry. It felt personal. These attacks took place around people and places that I knew!

Growing up, there was a certain store where I went to buy my candy. I frequented that store up the hill for over 3 years. I remember reading the owners' names in the paper in connection with the attacks. I felt betrayed. My uncle's brother worked at The World Trade Center. We could not find him for 48 hours.

I figured I would be deployed soon, but surprisingly, I didn't get deployment orders until 2003. When I came home with orders for Germany, I sat the kids down and told them we planned to move there. They were so excited about the prospect of seeing another country, but I had a feeling I was closer than ever to deployment.

Within 24 hours of arriving in Germany with my children, my supervisor called me into his office. He told me—while my children stood there waiting in the room—that the Army needed me in Iraq.

After I left his office, Malcolm, Jalisa, and Charlie started asking me all sorts of questions. *Mom, are you going to war? Are you going to get killed? Why do you have to go?* At this time, Malcolm was 11 and Jalisa was 10, while Charlie was only 6. Bombarded with so many questions, I felt frustrated that this announcement had been made in front of my kids. It was completely unprofessional.

"Can I please get 20 minutes to think?" I had asked them. I did not want to take my frustration out on them. So, I put on a poker face with a big smile.

"There is no need to worry," I lied. "You guys get to go back to the States and spend time with your friends. Once I get back from my seven-month deployment, I will fly to the States and bring you back to Germany."

I tried to reassure them. I told them that when I got back, we could travel Europe on my off days. That calmed them down a little. But I still worried, mostly about who would keep all three of my children. I wanted to keep them all together.

I felt especially fearful about who would take care of my daughter. I had lost touch with Sergeant Jones and his family after our divorce. I also did not have complete faith in my Family Care Plan. Amidst the concern about my children, I realized I felt very little concern about actually going to war.

Since the people on my Family Care Plan lived in the States, I had a week to get my children back to the U.S. before returning to Germany for training. But the people on my plan did not work out. I went through my phone directory and began calling people from A to Z. When this did not produce a single person willing to keep all of my children, I prepared myself to call Junior.

When I arrived back in the States two days later, my best friend, Linda—a former soldier— called me to tell me she wanted to keep all of the kids. Linda had just left active duty in the Army to join the National Guard. That meant she had the availability to look after them. She felt that their dad would not do a good job at keeping them since I had confided in her about Junior's actions when I left for Korea.

Although extremely grateful, I wondered about how well she would do. *Will she nurture my children or let them drive her crazy? Will she keep a careful watch with men around my daughter? Will she raise my children in a toxic environment?* I prayed she would act as a source of support. I prayed my children would trust her and feel safe. And at the very least, I prayed they would not fear telling me if something went wrong.

At some point after getting away from Specialist Abigor, I had begun to make friends and build a life at Fort Eustis, Virginia. Linda had participated in many of the "Friday functions" I had planned with my unit.

As an appointed First Sergeant, I had wanted my Fort Eustis soldiers to stay close and tight. I organized gatherings outside of work—things like bowling, skating, and dinners—that were still professional but also fostered family and fellowship amongst my soldiers. Linda and I gravitated to one another because we were both single, divorced mothers. She knew my pain.

"Having my three children is a lot of work, especially since you have three kids of your own," I explained to her over the phone. Linda had two girls around the same ages as Jalisa and Charlie and then an older son. Our kids had gone to school together.

"I don't think it'll be a problem. It's just seven months," Linda responded. I felt relieved that someone wanted to keep all three of my children together. The others I had reached out to kept offering to look after one child but not all. So, I said okay.

We went on to talk about how much I would pay her. With that out the way, we enrolled the children into school, in Powder Spring, Georgia where she had relocated and caught them up on their shots.

~

The day came for me to return to Germany. Linda and the children saw me off at the airport.

"You are leaving today. Why aren't you crying?" she asked me, "You won't see your children for seven months."

"I'm not going to cry in front of them. They're scared enough," I retorted.

I wanted them to see me as a strong woman. The stronger I looked, the easier the children would take my deployment to Iraq. Jalisa hugged me and would not let go. I tried to joke with her to get her spirits up. But once I turned around to leave, I never looked back. I could not. The tears finally fell, and I cried so much. I refused to let the children see me like that. I knew there was a chance I would come back in pieces or not at all.

They deployed me to Iraq for the first time around October of 2003, just a week after I returned to Germany. My unit had flown out there five months before me. With my children safely cared for, I had a little room for excitement. My pride to fight for our country conflicted with the guilt of leaving my children behind.

Touching down, I felt a rush of enthusiasm. I had joined the Army to keep us free. I finally had my chance to defend that freedom! This is what I spent my whole career training for!

We landed in Kuwait, a war-free zone, and took a convoy into Iraq. Seeing everybody in the convoy, synchronized and professional, impressed me.

On the drive, which took place at night, I gazed around in amazement. I had never seen so much sand! When I looked up in the sky, the moon looked so big. I could actually see Orion's Belt. I wanted to do everything, and I wanted to see everything. I had never traveled to the Middle East and felt curious to see the different ways people live around the world, just as I had done in Korea.

Now I feel like a soldier, I thought to myself as I took in my surroundings. The past 13 years in the Army had gone by much like a civilian job. I woke up, worked out, went to work, came home, took care of the kids, and did it all over again. Yet, suddenly, going to war felt meaningful.

12

Cultural Miscommunications

DURING MY TIME in Iraq, I observed that some of our cultural differences were just minor differences. And at other times, those differences could mean life or death.

For example, inside the city buildings, they made things like chandleries and faucets out of gold. These items had to be removed from the buildings at the introduction of American soldiers. I remember how vigorously U.S. Customs checked soldiers' luggage for gold. But I do not think the Iraqi people placed the high value on gold that we do in America. Kids who were the same age as my children begged for water.

In another incident, I questioned the Iraqis beliefs on gender. The Army worked alongside the Iraqi people against the insurgents. According to the battle plan, we went to the front of the village every morning at 0900 hours to pick up Iraqis to work for us. Typically, it was the same 15 Iraqi people. One of them was a self-elected supervisor who decided to act as a liaison for the whole 15 months we were in Iraq.

We paid those Iraqis to work with us during the daytime. These men worked on our plumbing and electrical systems. Or, they would bring supplies that we needed such as foam mattresses to put on our cots. Their role was basically helping to improve our quality of life within the forward operating base (FOB). These brave people risked their lives daily to help us because the insurgents would kill them if they found out.

I noticed after some time that the men who helped us always asked my male subordinates about their pay. They never communicated with me directly. Here I was, in the middle of a war wearing E-6 rank, and the Iraqi men refused to talk to me. They would only talk to my lower-enlisted *male* soldiers.

"Tell him, if he wants to get paid, to come and talk to me," I told my soldiers. But often the Iraqi men would choose to leave without pay rather than talk to me. This made me so mad! I felt furious every single time it happened. But I had to reflect on their culture and the fact that they also did not know our rank structure.

Then, there were the times when war became the realest for me. It weighed on me whenever I had to make choices that determined if and when people lived or died. Not anyone senior to me. ME!

On one such morning, we were patting down the workers to make sure they didn't have any contraband or weapons before getting into the five-ton trucks to get them through the checkpoint. Back then, we did not have much additional security. We were the security.

When doing our jobs, my soldiers and I always treated Iraqis with respect and dignity on these runs. I ensured that we all represented America well. So, we never had any problems picking up and dropping off the Iraqis before dark. Not once. But despite the structure and order in an Army day, danger still lurked in the desert dirt.

This chilly November day, a boy approached me. His Tuscany-leather-colored skin looked beat up by the harsh sun.

The boy was screaming. "La-a, La-a, La-a, La-a," he said repeatedly, which means "no." I took a step back and tried to put some space between us. He stepped closer. I watched the scabs on his cheeks rise and fall as he continued to shout, "La-a."

My maternal instincts wanted to reach for the child and give his skin a good scrub. As we stood eye to eye, I peered into his golden colored eyes. The soft brown shined brighter in contrast to the oily, matted jet-black hair. I had never seen him before and did not know who he belonged to. *What was his story? Did his family perish in the war? Was he an orphan? Were one of his parents among the villagers in the surrounding area?* I did not know, and I did not have the space or language to ask in those moments.

What I did know was that he was invading my space and causing a lot of attention. I felt scared and conflicted. I did not know his intentions and was frustrated by the communication barrier. He could have been a suicide bomber or a tactical distraction for another kind of attack.

I had heard about situations like this from other units. A lot of covert enemies would use the children as a distraction while others attacked a nearby target. The insurgents had used pregnant women in black dresses as a decoy; only, the women were not actually pregnant. There were weapons underneath their garments. These enemies were armed with explosives and ready to attack. My mind raced and my body reacted.

I pointed my weapon into the little boy's face. I did not plan to pull the trigger and really hoped he would not force me to. I just wanted him out of my face. I kept telling the young boy to move away. When words did not serve me and the body language did not translate, I hoped the threat would be enough.

My soldier, standing about six feet from me, noticed the tense situation with the boy. Next, the supervisor came to my aid. When he got closer, the boy started yelling, "Mister, Mister, one dollar."

The supervisor said something in Arabic and gestured the boy away. Finally, we headed back to our FOB.

On the drive back, I felt shaken. I thought about how much I did not want to hurt him, but I also did not want him hurting me or getting me sick. In my mind, I could see my son, Charlie, in that Iraqi boy. I will never forget the feeling of pointing my weapon at a child. For a quick moment I thought of Malcolm. (Years later, I found out that Specialist Abigor had pointed a gun to his head and threatened to kill us all.)

I silently thanked God that I was born in the land of the free, so my kids never had to live like the poor Iraqi people. I felt thankful my children were never desperate for necessities like water or food.

13

Tour Extended

AROUND MID-APRIL 2004, we prepared to leave Iraq. The morale was not high, but our focus stayed sharp. It had been seven months for me and 12 months for the rest of the brigade when we finally packed our containers. Part of the crew had already flown ahead to Hanau, Germany, in preparation for our arrival. Those of us still on the ground cleaned our weapons, suited up for protection, and inspected our vehicles. We got ready for our convoy from Iraq to Doha, Qatar.

The brigade vehicles were in two columns lined up in chalk order. Our five-ton, Old Lucy, was the third vehicle in the lineup. I prayed Old Lucy would not overheat or break down. The 959.5 miles we had to go were such a long way for Lucy. But my crew had done a good job conducting our weekly maintenance.

Everything looked good and Old Lucy passed all her safety checks, but I still felt extremely stressed. My mind would wander to terrifying visuals of getting hit or lost on the way to the city. In all the security reports I had read, the third vehicle in the convoy was always the one that would get hit. I hoped this concern was just my anxiety getting the best of me.

Night fall came. I packed the few belongings I had in my duffle bag and loaded it in the back of the five-ton. I headed towards our convoy briefing early to ensure all my soldiers arrived on time. I wanted more time to make any last-minute checks or adjustments. My heart raced and palms sweated, but my commanding bravado did not waver as everyone gathered for the briefing.

To our surprise, the top leaders had not gathered us to talk about the logistics of our next move. They informed us instead that the roads were not safe. We had to wait for the next night to leave. My encouraging words fell on deaf ears as bowed heads and slumped shoulders headed back to empty tents. They were understandably disappointed.

The next night turned into three nights. On the fourth night, the chaplain showed up. We knew immediately the news was dire. He announced that due to increased insurgent attacks and unrest, the Army extended our tour another three months. The Army needed our help getting the incoming division ready to take over the mission. They ordered those who had returned to Germany early to come back to Iraq.

Most soldiers became furious. Sadness mutated to depression and spread like a virus in the small community. Some leaders had to take weapons away from soldiers who had not taken the news well. I pulled my soldiers to the side for a more intimate conversation. A few of them refused to be comforted.

"You have no idea how it feels; you've only been here for seven months. We've been here for a year," they said. I let them vent and tried not to feel disrespected by their disappointment. I understood.

But they did not take my three children into consideration. I had to make sure this extension did not put my family in a terrible bind. None of my soldiers had children. I knew they could not understand or relate, so I kept it to myself.

~

"I need you to come and get these kids," Linda stated flatly. I gripped the phone receiver in one hand and put the other hand over my exasperated face. "Seven months is what we agreed on." "I'm in Iraq," I screamed into the receiver. "I can't just get on a plane and get them." My temperature rose to dangerous levels. Anger pained my chest and stifled my breathing.

Something had told me not to let her keep my kids, but had she seemed so sincere. *Leave them with me*, she said. *We will all have fun*, she said.

But there was nothing fun about having my time extended in the desert and trying to figure out who could take my kids next. Linda remained unwilling to keep my children for any additional amount of time. My Family Care Plan had failed. I was back to scrolling through my contacts to see who would look after my family.

I wondered again about how Linda had been treating my children. Was she abusing or mistreating them because she was stressed? I knew I had to hurry and remove them from an environment where they were not wanted. I asked her to give me a week to figure something out. It became my mission to place my children in a safe home for the rest of the Iraqi tour.

Then, I spoke to the kids. Their little pleas could penetrate even the thickest flak jacket.

"Mommy, you lied to us!" Charlie said.

"Chuckie, I know you're scared but the time will go by so fast!" I tried to console him. To sweeten the deal, I added, "And when I get to you, we are going to Euro Disney Resort!"

The other two frantically whispered their complaints. *She does not want us here anymore! We are always in trouble! She never takes us anywhere!*

I wanted to spare their feelings and tell them she did not really feel like that. I felt so much pressure and wondered if I was a bad mother for having left them there in the first place. I felt like I had abandoned them. If I could have taken them into my arms and held them, I could have made it right.

I did not know how to comfort them with so many miles between us. My explanation did not sound age appropriate. I could not tell them soldiers were dying. I just had to keep my composure. I held in my tears and told them how much I loved them.

"I'm so sorry that the plans changed," I managed. I left the phone center to go to my tent and on the way there I struggled for each breath. I just kept hearing those sweet little voices begging me to come rescue them. My heart broke for my children.

One of the medics found me lying on the ground, gasping for air. He picked me up and carried me about 200 yards to the Aids Station and told me I was having an asthma attack. The Army issued me an inhaler.

I spent the next three days making calls until someone agreed to keep all three of my kids. McKay, a First Sergeant, and battle buddy I served with in Virginia, agreed to help. She, Linda, and I had all been stationed at Fort Eustis, Virginia together. We had all hung out a few times. McKay would crash on my couch when she did not feel like taking the long drive home from work. We often helped each other out.

She had just returned from deploying herself, so we knew there was little chance she would deploy again soon. It almost felt rude to ask for this favor because I knew that, after returning from her own tour in Iraq, she probably wanted to take leave.

First Sergeant McKay did not have kids; she focused solely on her career. She was three years my senior, two pay grades ahead, and a high achiever compared to her peers. She had cared for my children sometimes when I worked late. First Sergeant McKay had helped the kids with homework and frequently bought them toys or clothes. I always knew she would be a good mom if she chose.

When I called Linda back to let her know First Sergeant McKay would meet her to retrieve the children, she sounded sour. Then, she told me she needed more money before First Sergeant McKay picked them up because the kids had gotten too expensive for her. I sent her the money for two reasons: I didn't want to take any further risk while Linda still had my kids in her care, and I really did feel grateful that she had cared for them up to that point. I thanked her for all she had done for us.

A week later, I sent First Sergeant McKay the money to purchase a round-trip ticket to Germany for herself and one-way tickets for the kids. She flew to the States, into Atlanta, Georgia packed up my children, and flew back to Germany. When I called her to see how the trip had gone, she told me that Linda had a new car. That raised our suspicions about how she had been using the money I sent her for the kids.

I gave First Sergeant McKay full power of attorney to handle all matters relating to my family. And I decided to just focus on my relief that the kids had arrived in Germany in good hands.

14

No Place for Romance

A 5'9" BRONZE FIGURE strutted around the Bob Hope Dining Facility. My eyes followed, despite myself, and I was not as discreet as I thought. My soldiers reported a smile on my face every time he came around. They said I would glow. I thought no one else knew about the butterflies in my stomach. I dropped my head so they would not see the blush creep in my cheeks.

He had my attention, but I did not plan to offer him much more than that. We were in Iraq. I had to focus on the mission, and I was not there for anything else. The desert is no place for feelings. Leave feelings for the phone or letter home. Fillings are for holes in teeth. Fillings are for pleasant surprises in a pastry. But not for soldiers at war.

I was always mentally and physically tired after working 16-hour shifts or ducking, dodging, and swerving explosives on convoys. I felt exhausted and looked dusty from all the sand. I nearly melted from heat greater than 130 degrees every day. Most days after work, I just wanted to relax, detach, and jump in a refrigerator or something.

Specialist Anthony was a ray of sunshine in the madness of war. He always found a way to show up wherever I might be—so much so that I got used to seeing him. And if I could not see him, he would leave sweet notes or my favorite candy on top of my pillow on my cot. It had been over two years since I had divorced Sergeant Jones and even longer since I had been in a real relationship. I proceeded slowly and cautiously.

On nights that we actually had free time, we would all meet at my tent to talk and play spades or dominos. The more I hung out with Specialist Anthony, the more I realized he was not as ambitious as I would have liked. Ultimately, I set a goal for myself to be a Command Sergeant Major. He was not even trying for the next rank. But I figured if he stuck around me and my group, our ambition might rub off on him. In time, I believed Specialist Anthony gained more focus, started to apply my advice, and made a better soldier and man.

~

Our battalion did regular health and welfare inspections to ensure all soldiers followed regulations. During the inspections they looked for any contraband, such as alcohol, drugs, pornography, stolen weapons, souvenirs, or artifacts that could be sold for profit in the States.

On one such inspection, while I had my card crew in my tent, I found out—or should I say the whole battalion found out—that soldiers weren't allowed to have soldiers of the opposite sex in their tents. This surprised me, especially because when I first moved into my tent, two *male* soldiers lived on the other side of the same tent.

They wrote me up that night for having Specialist Anthony in my tent even though none of us had ever heard of these regulations until then. Since I was the most senior person living in the tent, the First Sergeant made me responsible. I felt devastated, hurt, and betrayed by the Chain of Command.

The next day, Specialist Anthony's First Sergeant came to me and told me I would be under investigation for getting involved with a married soldier. He suggested I fight the charges because he had never heard of these regulations until then either.

Those accusations could have gotten me kicked out of the Army. I felt blindsided. First, I never even knew Specialist Anthony was married. Second, we were not even dating; we were all just friends hanging out in my tent. We tried just for one moment to have some safe fun. And it backfired.

The accusation of fraternization came down directly from my First Sergeant. The flag on my record made me ineligible for promotions, prevented me from attending school, and stopped me from reenlisting.

I racked my brain for the reasons for this humiliation. I had been a stellar soldier for my entire career. As I flipped through my thoughts like a photo album, I did not like what I landed on.

I recalled the time my First Sergeant invited me to share a care package he had received in the mail. He had wine-bottle-shaped chocolate candies filled with liquor. I loved chocolate, so I indulged. But I did not drink alcohol, so I felt the effects of the liquor rapidly.

My First Sergeant had laughed at how I had gotten drunk off chocolate candy. Then, he rubbed my arms and told me to take a nap.

"I have to get back to the office," I slurred.

"No, you're good. Just go take a nap," he had said. I went back to my tent and slept through dinner that night.

This First Sergeant was the same person who accused me of fraternization. I found out later that Specialist Anthony had shown my First Sergeant his divorce decree months earlier. Yet, my First Sergeant took his sweet time removing the charges and stopping the investigation and removing my flag. I concluded that my First Sergeant may have been jealous about where my attention had turned. There really was nothing to investigate. Specialist Anthony was not married, and we were not a couple. My whole career depended on my First Sergeant doing the right thing.

After a month, the investigation came back innocent. My First Sergeant finally dropped the charges and lifted the flag after six months. But he never apologized for putting me through the embarrassment and almost ending my career.

15

On the Road Again

JULY OF 2004 could not come fast enough. During the three-month extension, I suffered a Traumatic Brain Injury (TBI). Every morning- even if we got hit with IED, the tents caught on fire, or if the Messiah returned- we had PT at 0530 hours. I felt like I zombie as I pushed my tired body to the front of the motor pool. When all the troops were present and accounted for, we headed down the road on a run.

I pushed my left foot in front of the right foot and caught the rhythm alongside my soldiers. Without warning, as I was running backwards to check on my soldiers I tumbled, and my skull met the paved road. The blow was so severe I was medically evacuated to the nearest hospital in Baghdad International Airport (BIAP), in a helicopter.

Twenty-four hours later, I called my Chain of Command and begged them to send a convoy to pick me up. I knew I was not completely healed, but I could not stay there a minute longer. The time was coming for us to go home.

Once again, it was time to pack up, get our vehicles lined up, and prepare for convoy. Night fell and we received our safety briefing. So many emotions sped through me. I felt nervous but elated at the thought of getting home to my children soon.

The convoy extracting us from Iraq turned out to be the scariest thing I had ever seen or done. At 0200 hours, my clothes clung to my skin from sweat. I looked down for a second to grab some water. Suddenly, I saw bullets firing through the air; the tracers attached left blazing trails overhead like deadly fireflies.

The First Sergeant called on the radio and issued a command to dismount and start shooting. This was not how we had been trained to respond, but I passed the command on to the soldiers. I told them to dismount but keep the door open as we returned fire into the darkness before us. I could tell by the distance that these bullets were intended for a different convoy. Our group was not in imminent danger. We should have been leaving.

Just as suddenly, they ordered us to get back in our vehicles. I jumped in the driver's side and yelled for my soldier to jump in. We watched as other soldiers ran to get back in their moving vehicles. It all happened so fast.

At the safe zone, we realized all our soldiers survived but some of the civilians died that night. We stayed at the safe zone for a day, waiting for clearance to get back on the road. Once we arrived in Camp Doha, Kuwait, we stayed for two days before boarding planes to Germany.

My children came to the hanger at Hanau, Germany, to welcome me home. It felt like Christmas morning and my children were the gifts under the tree!

The command hosted a big ceremony for the returning soldiers. We entered the hangar and filed into formation. Our friends and family watched us from the bleachers as they cheered and held up signs. My kids made one that read, "We love you mom." The presentation was beautiful, and the appreciation felt good. But really, I longed for rest.

When I hugged my children after the ceremony, they felt so unfamiliar to me. They had grown so much. Everybody looked a few inches taller—especially Malcolm. I had to look up to meet his big brown eyes. Jalisa and I stood shoulder to shoulder now. And my baby boy, Charlie … well, he was still fun-sized. I marveled at how much they changed and thanked God we made it back safely to each other.

As much as I wanted to sleep, there is no rest for the working single mother who must get her house back in order. I felt heavy with responsibility. The house in Germany was empty. I had not lived there long enough to fill it. My first night back, we ate fast food because I had no pots to cook with and there was no food in the house.

There were other parts about reacclimating that no one had told me about. None of the Army's safety briefings prepared me for the dangers of my own mind. I would sometimes wake up in the middle of the night feeling confused about where I was. I would jump out of the bed looking for my weapon. For 10 months, I had kept my weapon with me through everything. It was either on my back, under the mattress of my cot, or in reaching distance while I took a shower. I felt vulnerable without it. Other nights, I stayed up crying with a heavy sense of loneliness.

After a deployment, the Army's integration process required eight days of formal training intended to help soldiers' transition smoothly from a war zone to domestic life. It would take a lot more than eight days to erase the dark memories and get back to normal. What I saw and did was too much for any one human being to see or endure.

Spouses in the Army had Command-Sponsored Family Readiness Groups to assist with these transitions. The group leaders would help group members communicate with the spouses of soldiers returning from war. They gave suggestions and guidelines for how to discuss difficult questions and sensitive information. But the Army did not provide any resources for my children to understand what I had gone through.

Kids do not have a filter. They boldly blasted me with their questions about war. They asked me so many questions that I did not think they would ever ask me, many of which I was not ready to answer!

The most intrusive question: "Mom, did you kill anybody?" I felt uneasy with the excitement in their tones. Maybe they thought it was cool. And I did not know how to explain all the reasons it was not.

The questions they asked drove a wedge between us. Even though my kids needed me so much, I separated myself from them. At times I would just stay in my room. I could not be the fun mother they once knew and loved. Once again, I felt trapped between two entirely different worlds. It was more difficult than ever before to merge the two. Iraq had changed me forever.

FOUR

The Final Destination

16

From House to Home?

THE HOME IN Fliegerhorst Kaserne, Germany, was not a familiar place because I had deployed so soon after we moved. Starting our lives together there felt like we had hit the reset button on life. The house had no furniture, we had no car, and I did not know anything about the local currency or exchange rate.

Specialist Anthony, however, had been in Germany before. He offered to show me around and help me get familiar with my surroundings. Everyone else I knew who had been living there had left for leave. Hanau Army Airfield looked like a ghost town with most of the soldiers gone.

While everyone enjoyed their leave, Specialist Anthony and I spent most of our days together. It would have been easy to rush into a dating situation since we had so few distractions. He definitely expressed his interest in dating me, but it seemed like I could only keep my head above water. Specialist Anthony was so energetic, and I was just so ... depressed. I began to think if I dated him, maybe I could swipe away this dark cloud over my head. I thought he could fix the brokenness inside me.

The Battalion held a BBQ once everyone returned from leave. It was our first time getting everyone back together after 30 days. Specialist Anthony and I decided this would be a good opportunity to introduce him to the kids. Once I arrived at the BBQ with them, I introduced the children to my soldiers, let them get food, and freed them to have a good time. Then, when Specialist Anthony's eyes met mine, I told my kids I had someone special I wanted them to meet. They already knew what "special" meant. I called Specialist Anthony over and introduced him to my family.

"What would you say if I was dating him?" I asked the children when he had left. They told me he seemed cool and they wanted to invite him over to the house to play video games. By the end of the night, they were singing his praises.

After six more months of dating, Specialist Anthony and I got engaged. He asked the kids for their permission first. They looked so happy when he proposed. I was not sure if saying yes was the right decision, but I thought if I married him, I would be less depressed. Two months later, we got married at the courthouse and signed the marriage certificate there.

~

Soon after I married Specialist Anthony, I found out the Army selected me for the Sergeant First Class list. I needed someone to watch the children for 10 weeks while I attended Advance Noncommissioned Officer Course (ANCOC). I felt more at ease about having childcare options right there in Germany. I felt some reservation about Specialist Anthony looking after the children by himself for ten weeks so early into our marriage but having our support system would make his life easier. Soldiers would come by almost in a rotation to watch the kids whenever Specialist Anthony needed help. I went away to training fully focused and ready to learn.

Upon my return, I found out my husband had cheated on me with some of my own soldiers. To make matters worse, a letter came in the mail addressed to him. It was from a woman with his last name. I knew it was against the law, but I opened the letter anyway. The letter revealed he had never actually gotten divorced. When I confronted him, he admitted to altering the divorce decree he showed to my First Sergeant. The divorce decree originally belonged to his older brother, but he changed the name on it.

Although I was furious, I was also exhausted, overwhelmed, and tired of putting my children through so many changes. I stayed with Sergeant Anthony and decided to work it out.

17

Fort Riley—911

SIX MONTHS AFTER returning from my first deployment to Iraq and my assignment to Hanau, Germany. I received orders to head to Fort Riley, Kansas. After only six months there, I received orders for a second tour in Iraq. It felt like, for the last three years, all we did was pack and unpack. And it was time to pack again for the second deployment.

A small group of us hung around in the office joking and laughing, waiting around for the last formation of the day at 1700 hours. I had finished packing our container in preparation for Iraq. The phone rang and my soldier answered it.

"Sergeant First Class Davis," he said. "It's for you." His tone shook with concern.

"Who is it?" I asked.

"The MP's station." MP stood for Military Police. The whole office became silent when I retrieved the phone from my soldier.

I answered quietly out of fear and discretion. "This is Sergeant First Class Davis. How can I help you?"

The officer immediately assured me that my son was okay but let me know there had been an incident. "Your son, Malcolm, fainted and stopped breathing. He is okay now, but he was taken to the hospital." I dropped the phone and yelled that my son was in the hospital and that I needed to go. I did not give them any other information. Speeding toward St. Jude Hospital in Topeka, Kansas, I felt terrified. I knew it was not rational, but I was afraid that, when I got to the hospital, I would get the worst news a mother could get.

I called my husband, Sergeant Anthony, but he didn't seem as concerned or worried as I was. I cried all the way through the 45-minute drive.

I parked in the first spot available, ran through the hospital doors, and hurled inquiries at the front desk nurse.

"What room is my son in?" I repeated. She asked his name in a calm professional tone.

I shouted, "Malcolm! Please help me." She typed his name in the computer, walked me to his room, and told me to calm down.

"He is okay. He is breathing fine. As a matter of fact, he is quite the charmer," she said. Charmer was an understatement. When I walked into his room, Malcolm was laughing and having a good time with the nurses.

Malcolm had been running at track practice when he unexpectedly fainted and lost consciousness. He had not been breathing so the doctors had to use a defibrillator on him. The doctors had waited on me to give him his diagnosis: a heart condition called Long QT Syndrome. It is a lifelong condition of the heart. The symptoms include abnormal heartbeats that can lead to death. He had to make some drastic lifestyle changes: no more sports or strenuous exercising and he had to take medication for the rest of his life.

The news took a toll on him. My heart broke for my oldest son as I watched him crying and feeling hopeless. Basketball and track had become important parts of how he navigated and coped in his world.

On the ride back home from the hospital, I rehearsed in my head how I would ask my Battalion Command Sergeant Major to get out of the orders for another deployment to Iraq. When I dropped Malcolm off at the house, I went straight to my office. I explained my son's chronic health condition and asked for reassignment to the rear detachment unit so that I could take care of my son.

"No. That's not possible," he said. "You are essential personnel in this deployment."

I would have to tell Malcolm I was soon deploying once more, this time for 15 months, on top of the news he had already received. On the way home, I rehearsed the words again in my head.

We talked and I explained to Malcolm that I had done everything I could to get out of this deployment. I told him that I loved him very much and that I was so sorry for everything going on. I promised him that when I got back, we would do more family trips.

I also told him he could get his license and I would purchase a car for his 17th birthday. (Maybe I was trying to bribe him?) I just did not want him thinking I did not care. I did not want him to feel unloved or that I did not try hard enough to get out of going to war.

The conversation ended with me reminding him about how much he liked computers. I encouraged him to explore that while his body healed. I wanted him to have hope in his time of need. I was not sure if he was okay mentally after passing out and getting resuscitated, then receiving so much bad news in one day. It would have been a lot for anyone, and this was my son.

18

Operation Iraqi Freedom: Part II

FOR SERGEANT ANTHONY and I to work through our differences, we both agreed it was necessary for him to get legally divorced. He did. Then, we got married again—the right way this time. I believed this gave him an opportunity to show up in the marriage differently than he had before.

Our first wedding had been a proxy wedding. After returning from my first deployment, the battalion had sent me to Fort Hood, Texas, for "temporary duty" (TDY), for 45 days to help with the battalion deactivation. During that time, Sergeant Anthony and I had agreed on a proxy wedding; he was not physically present. One of his old friends, who was stationed at Fort Hood, Texas, stood in his place to be a witness for my soon-to-be husband.

I hoped hearing him tell me he would be faithful and would change things. I hoped I would feel better and things would get better. He was good with the kids only when it was time to play. He never had it in him to discipline the kids. The kids loved him because, to them, he was just a big kid. I hoped we had solidified our commitment to one another, especially since deployment reared its ugly head again at the top of the year in 2007. I shifted my focus to finding someone to watch my children for my next tour in Iraq.

Although I had a spouse, we were both deploying, so I still needed a Family Care Plan. I had only met Sergeant Anthony's family once and I did not want to ask them for help. The children were also older, so they had more opinions about where they wanted to go.

Malcolm informed me he had been talking to his father and paternal grandmother on Myspace. He had not seen his grandmother since he was about four years old but had found comfort in their new relationship. Then, Malcolm requested to stay with his father when I left for Iraq.

I told him I needed to think about it. I did not know anything about Junior's living arrangements or his financial status. And he was $8,000 in arrears on child support. I really needed someone responsible who would ensure Malcolm took his meds daily, keep a close eye on him, and make sure he did not overexert himself.

I tried Malcolm and Jalisa's paternal grandmother first. I called her and asked if she could keep both of her grandchildren while I deployed to Iraq. Without even a thought or hesitation, she said no!

"Okay," I responded and swiftly hung up the phone. I felt humiliated asking for help and getting denied. She never displayed the love and concern a grandma should and never really got involved in her grandchildren's lives. So, I was not surprised. It just hurt to have to tell my son and daughter that their grandmother did not want to keep them. But Malcolm still wanted to live with his father while I was away. I called Junior next and, as usual, he agreed to keep Malcolm if I paid him. I felt outraged that his care for his children was so conditional. I agreed to let Malcolm stay there but Jalisa had begun to fill out and look more like a lady. Because of my past history of sexual abuse, I felt more comfortable with Jalisa staying with a female than her own dad. I would have to make additional arrangements for her.

Malcolm had also managed to find Sergeant Jones, Charlie's dad, on Myspace. We had started talking again on the phone nearly every day. He expressed his happiness that Malcolm had found him. He had gotten married again and had a new son.

He asked to keep Charlie for the summer, and I told him we needed care sooner because of an upcoming deployment. Sergeant Jones agreed right away! I offered to pay him, and Sergeant Jones just agreed to whatever I said. Charlie and Sergeant Jones could not wait to see one another. Sergeant Jones had always treated the children kindly and gently, so I trusted Charlie would be fine.

That left Jalisa. I dipped into my sisterhood to find someone who could keep Jalisa for the entire 15 months. I landed on my friend Porsha who lived in Richmond, Virginia. We had served in Iraq together and had become good friends in Germany. Porsha was a single mom who had a four-year-old daughter. I would watch her daughter when she would go to the field or when she had 24-hour duty. With this situation, Jalisa could even babysit when needed.

Porsha worked as an instructor at the Advanced Individual Training schoolhouse in Fort Lee, Virginia. Her job made her less likely to be given deployment orders.

~

This time, I deployed to Iraq as a married woman. Not too many people can say they fought a war in Iraq with their spouse. In the brigade there might have been a handful of other married soldiers like us. It was bittersweet. Of course, I felt bitter about leaving my children behind for 15 months but thankful to fight alongside my husband.

At work, I felt more confident as a senior non-commissioned officer who had deployed to Iraq before. I understood the risks and the circumstances. Still, having my husband with me presented a new set of challenges. I worried about his safety, and I also worried if he would cheat on me with the women in his unit. This concern felt both personal and professional since we were all in the same brigade. The never-ending worries about him, the kids, and my junior soldiers left me mentally drained.

My husband lived in a different tent city than the one I lived in. His tent city was about a quarter of a mile distance from mine. We saw each other only at night about three times a week. Whenever an incident occurred, of course I worried about Sergeant Anthony. But I had to ensure the safety of my soldiers first. The Army required that he be last on my list of priorities. Sometimes I had to wait hours before hearing from him to make sure he and his soldiers were safe.

~

Once we returned from Iraq, Sergeant Anthony went away for his own 10-week-long advanced courses. While he was not around, I found out he had been taking advantage of a 16-year-old girl. My heart simply could not take it anymore. I would not risk him looking at my daughter's friends. Jalisa had also just turned 16 at the time. I refused to enable my husband to abuse my daughter the way my mother had allowed her husband to take advantage of me.

When I told the children about my plans to divorce Sergeant Anthony, Charlie was devastated. Jalisa and Malcolm understood, but Charlie cried and blamed me for everything. "It's your fault," Charlie cried, "You should forgive him."

Charlie quietly kept in touch with Sergeant Anthony for a while after the divorce. He would call Sergeant Anthony to pick him up after school and they would talk about me. Charlie was too young to understand and I did not want to share more details of my personal life with him as a child.

I wanted my children to stay kids. They should not have to worry so much about adult issues. But I guess I could not hide it from them any longer. Another failed marriage.

19

Fallen Soldiers

It seemed the Grim Reaper deployed with us to Iraq in 2007. My first day there, death greeted me in the form of a conversation with a former battle buddy. We were catching up and he casually mentioned a mutual friend of ours had died in a car accident. When he saw the tears, I tried to hold back, he apologized. He thought I already knew. I said a prayer for our comrade's wife and son. I regrouped to put my feelings in check because, of course, the mission had to keep going.

Ten months into the deployment, my heart shattered again. I lost one of *my* soldiers to suicide —a 26-year-old man with two children and a wife—in the most painfully violent way. I felt full responsibility for Specialist Blue's death. It was my duty to serve and protect my soldiers, but I had failed at my mission.

The First Sergeant put me in charge of cleaning his remains. My hands touched his brain matter. Blood decorated the walls, floor, and ceiling, and the smell of it was still thick in the air hours after the fatal incident. I finished gathering his belongings to send back to his family. Finally, I went back to my living area.

Alone in my room, I began to break down. I cried. I felt anger, guilt, and grief. There were so many emotions all at once. I took pride in making sure my soldiers were the best at what they did. And I had been really hard on him. *Maybe that's why Specialist Blue did not come to confide in me about how he was feeling or what he was going through.*

The next few mornings, we stood in formation as usual. Three times, they called his name during roll call. The rhythm of battle paused as his name echoed in the wind. Of course, he did not answer. Death—after all—is the only legitimate reason for missing formation. And I felt his loss more deeply than I had felt any other.

A couple of days later, my CSM came to my living area. His driver knocked on my door. When I opened it, he could tell that I was not taking my soldier's death well.

"Get your weapon," he said. "I am personally taking you to see a military counselor."

"I'm good, Sergeant Major," I said.

"If you do not get in this vehicle, I will have the military police take you." He gave me no choice but to grab my weapon and get in the vehicle. Even though I felt embarrassed and concerned that his driver might tell someone what he overheard, I complied and went to the doctor's office.

I saw the counselor for two days and then quit. I took one look at that man in his stiff, clean uniform and I knew I did not trust him. His demeanor reminded me of the men I had worked with before: rude and lackluster in emotion. I had hoped these old farts had retired or gotten out by then. This man had no compassion for my loss or the weight of the guilt I felt. He responded dryly to everything I confided. He shrugged off my junior soldier's death and advised me to do the same since Specialist Blue was not killed by enemy fire.

I never told the counselor that the night before I lost Specialist Blue, we had done karaoke. I got on the stage and sang a duet with one of my soldiers. Specialist Blue got on stage and sang a song as well. Many soldiers got on stage, even the First Sergeant.

Once everybody left, I went to my housing container, sat in a chair, and stared at my Army-issued M4 weapon. The weapon called to me. I took it in my hands and placed the barrel inside of my mouth. The cold salty metal met my throat and I closed my eyes to brace for the impact. I felt ready, excited even, for the kiss of death. I was tired of living with so much pain.

But before I got my finger around the trigger, someone knocked at my door. My cheating husband had stopped by to check on me. Deep down, I think my soldier's death made me jealous. He was the courageous one. I was stuck here.

~

Four months after I returned home from my second deployment, I started getting back in touch with friends. I had taken some time to reacclimate myself to the States before calling anyone. I understood better that I needed time to transition back into domestic mode.

When I called my friend SFC Jack to vent about my latest assignment, I found out he died of a heart attack. SFC Jack had been my go-to guy whenever I needed someone to listen. We had met in training at Fort Lee, Virginia, back in 2005. We used to ride together to class every day back then. After that, we had kept in touch through the years and duty stations.

It had been a while since I reached out because of my deployment. I dialed his number only to be informed that he had passed away.

That day, I decided not to have any more friends. I was tired of losing my friends. I could not take another loss.

20

～～～◦◦～～～

Pack It Up and Go Home!

T HE SECOND TOUR of Iraq concluded with an
awards ceremony to observe stellar soldiers'
achievements during Operation Iraqi Freedom 2007
to 2009. I was surprised to be among the awardees.
The Army awarded me the Bronze Star—the fourth
highest individual military award.

I stood awkwardly among the officers and
scanned the crowd of my peers and subordinates. My
eyes landed on the gap in the ranks where Specialist
Blue would have been. My heart sank for him and
his family. My heart sank for my family as I thought
about how much my children had endured while I
was at war.

I felt so many mixed emotions. My chest swelled
with pride as the commanding officer described how
I "distinguished myself in a heroic way above all my

peers." I fought for my country because I loved to do it. But no amount of training could prepare me for the sacrifices I had to make to get there. A part of me felt like I should not leave Iraq, since I could not bring all my soldiers back with me. The guilt made me sick to my stomach.

After the ceremony, I reached out to my children. I wanted to share the good news with them. I did not get a word in because Linda had asked me to come and get my children immediately. She had taken over as the kids' caretaker instead of Porsha, Junior, and Sergeant Jones in the midst of my deployment. I explained to her that I only had four weeks left but that did not stop her from wanting me to get them.

I told her to give me a couple of days. I developed a plan that I knew would work. Our battalion needed several people to go back two weeks early. I asked my Command Sergeant Major if I could be included in those numbers. He said yes but he also made it clear that I had to go straight to work.

Next, I arranged for the kids to arrive in Kansas a day before I did. I was friends with one of the soldiers' wives, who agreed to pick them up from the airport. They stayed with her overnight and she brought them to the welcome ceremony. When I arrived at Fort Riley, Kansas, my children were waiting for me with open arms.

I felt so overjoyed to see them. No matter what I put them through, they still loved me. I just hoped one day they would see that all my sacrifice was for them and our country.

21

Looking Back to Move Forward

BEING IN THE Army as a minority and a single mother, I fought for every ounce of respect I received. When I started my military career, there was nothing else I could imagine myself doing. By the end of it, I was mentally, emotionally, and physically drained.

I gave up. I did not want to keep fighting the battle for mutual respect in a world that only pretended to respect all soldiers. In many instances, I felt unsafe when surrounded by unfamiliar men because I had been sexually violated before and during my time in the Army. When it came to my orders and assignments, that fear did not even matter. Nor did my rank.

I had signed up to be in a man's world. These men had done things a certain way their entire careers. *Who was I to change their minds? Who was I to change their world?* I concluded the Army was no place for women. I just wanted to put my burdens down to go be a stay-at-home mom.

Sitting at home with my children, I realized it was they who had actually made the ultimate sacrifice. Every time I came back from deployment, my children acted out in various ways. Eventually I realized lashing out was their way of expressing their feelings about my continued absence over the years.

And it was not just my children acting out. I remember one of the times Malcolm got in trouble with the law, my supervisor told me his daughter was also in trouble with the law. My supervisor also had a boss whose son had tried to commit suicide. Another of my colleagues' sons had gone to prison. All of these children were around 16 to 18 years old and many of them either got in trouble with the law or wanted to end their lives.

As I grappled with my own diagnosis with PTSD, I wondered if my children—if all of our children— suffered from PTSD as well. Each of my children most definitely showed the symptoms at one point or another. They struggled with their own fear, agony, depression, insomnia, and anxiety. Over the years, I watched them endure everything—from the fear of losing me to getting bounced around from person to person like foster children. I know those feelings took their toll.

Malcolm struggled a lot during my absence during my first deployment. He got caught shoplifting at Walmart. He told me he did it in hopes that it would bring me home from the war sooner during my first deployment. He did not know how to really express to me how he felt. It wasn't until he was in his early 20's that Malcolm and I were able to talk about this.

Thankfully, we had some heart-to-heart conversations before he was shot and killed. He told me that he understood why I had not been there and that he was proud of what I had done for my country. Still, he also said that he wished he had grown up with more hugs and kisses.

I had not been the most affectionate mother to my kids. I have stated before that the Army really doesn't equip or encourage us to deal with our emotions as some other professions do. I continue to be a work of progress in this area of my life.

Jalisa has been more vocal about expressing her feelings of isolation, loneliness, and her fears of growing up without me when I was deployed. So, we had come up with a special secret word—a word that we could use in any conversation. The word was only supposed to be used if she felt danger or she had been harmed in any way. We were the only two people who knew the secret word.

If she ever used the word, I knew exactly what to do. I would either call the cops or get to her as soon as I could. She also understood that there was no right or wrong way of using the word. If she felt unsafe, I had told her to not hesitate and that there were no consequences for using the secret word. This made us both feel safe or at least relieved that we could speak in codes and help would be on the way. We still use that word today.

It was difficult for her being away from her brothers. She was a daddy's girl. Growing up without her father was hard on her. She was also extremely hard on herself; no matter how many times I told her she was smart and pretty, she would say, "You have to say that. You are my mother."

Maybe because of my absent or her father's absent she developed this self-critical behavior, making her feel inadequate in spite of her outer and inner beauty and her intellect. Like any other girl, she always needed her father.

Was it my fault staying in the Army or that she did not have a father? I often asked myself those questions. Her confidence in her own ability was low. She always questioned her success. She was presented with the MVP award her senior year in high school, but she still had doubts about her own abilities.

I always felt guilty for leaving Jalisa because she always wanted her dad to be around. Whenever I left for long periods of time, she really felt alone. Sometimes I think I made bad choices with men in hopes of providing her with a dad. Sometimes I felt like I was shopping for a dad. And sometimes I was so depressed I had no idea what I was thinking or doing. But I learned the hard way that I could not find them or buy them a dad. I had missed key moments in her life like her first words and steps.

Charlie, to this day, recounts how he cried himself to sleep every night I was on deployment because I was not there to put him to bed. I think his biggest fear was that I could die at war. When he was old enough, he also had to deal with the truth about his biological father and what Specialist Abigor had done to me. He has also had his own troubles with the law.

Seeing my children's pain so clearly these days, I wonder how many other children are suffering. Have Americans considered the difficult plight of military children? If someone did a survey, how many military children would qualify for a diagnosis of severe PTSD? What programs and services do we have in place for them? I have a heart for these children suffering in silence. I wrote this book to help bring attention to their stories.

In the future, I hope to see progress in the way the military treats its female soldiers as well as in how they handle sexual reports. I hope they will develop programs to help children deal with life during the seasons that their parents are deployed, as well as after deployment.

I have seen the courage, bravery, and resilience of so many soldiers and their families. I pray that one day we can all be the heroes for ourselves that we were for our country.

THE END

About The Author

VICKI **DAVIS**, former soldier in the U.S. Army, retired after 21 years and 11 months of active services as a senior noncommissioned officer. Serving two tours in Iraq. While in Operation Iraqi Freedom, she received the Bronze Star Medal for her extraordinary act of valor. Furthermore, she graduated from Saint Leo University with a bachelor's degree in criminal justices.

A survivor of gun violence and a courageous single mother who managed even through her adversities to be resourceful while wearing multiple hats as a Mother, Soldier, Leader, and Friend; these hats define who she is as a person who risks her life for our country.

Made in the USA
Columbia, SC
25 August 2020